ISBN 978-1-333-02772-8
PIBN 10454620

1 MONTH OF
FREE
READING

at
www.ForgottenBooks.com

By purchasing this book you are eligible for one month membership to ForgottenBooks.com, giving you unlimited access to our entire collection of over 1,000,000 titles via our web site and mobile apps.

To claim your free month visit:
www.forgottenbooks.com/free454620

English
Français
Deutsche
Italiano
Español
Português

www.forgottenbooks.com

Mythology Photography **Fiction**
Fishing Christianity **Art** Cooking
Essays Buddhism Freemasonry
Medicine **Biology** Music **Ancient**
Egypt Evolution Carpentry Physics
Dance Geology **Mathematics** Fitness
Shakespeare **Folklore** Yoga Marketing
Confidence Immortality Biographies
Poetry **Psychology** Witchcraft
Electronics Chemistry History **Law**
Accounting **Philosophy** Anthropology
Alchemy Drama Quantum Mechanics
Atheism Sexual Health **Ancient History**
Entrepreneurship Languages Sport
Paleontology Needlework Islam
Metaphysics Investment Archaeology
Parenting Statistics Criminology
Motivational

tou
Maj. Genl's

OUR NATIONAL FL

THE STARS AND ST

ITS HISTORY IN A CENTUI

ADDRESS DELIVERED BEFORE THE NEW YORK HIST(
JUNE 14TH, 1877, THE CENTENNIAL OF THE AI
THE STARS AND STRIPES AS OUR NATIONA

BY

MAJOR-GENL. SCHUYLER HAMIL

OUR NATIONAL FLAG;

THE STARS AND STRIPES;

ITS HISTORY IN A CENTURY.

ADDRESS DELIVERED BEFORE THE NEW YORK HISTORICAL SOCIETY,
JUNE 14TH, 1877, THE CENTENNIAL OF THE ADOPTION OF
THE STARS AND STRIPES AS OUR NATIONAL FLAG;

BY

MAJOR-GENL. SCHUYLER HAMILTON.

Compliments of

MAJOR-GENERAL SCHUYLER HAMILTON.

NEW YORK:

GEORGE R. LOCKWOOD,

No. 812 BROADWAY.

1877.

OUR NATIONAL FLAG,

THE STARS AND STRIPES.

___

ITS HISTORY IN A CENTURY.

___

Mr. President and Members of the New York Historical Society.

LADIES AND GENTLEMEN :—I shall waste no portion of the limited time in which I can hope to engage your attention, on a subject more than co-extensive with the history of the nation during a century, in apologies as to the manner in which I have endeavored to execute the pleasant task which, through your kindness, has been devolved upon me.

In 1853, in compliance with a request of Lieut.-General Winfield Scott, prompted by an inquiry made to him by the Hon. Daniel Webster, Secretary of State, that a satisfactory reply might be made to a Foreign Minister, who desired to be informed of the origin and meaning of the devices combined in the National Flag of the United States of America, I prepared and published a monograph on the subject. The late Hon. Charles Sumner quoted from it on the floor of the United States Senate, and the conclusions I then arrived at have, I think, met with general acceptance.

The United States of America as a nation is the daughter of Great Britain. The National Flag of the United States is, therefore, naturally derived from the National Flag of the Mother country.

Our National Flag is very often called the Star Spangled Banner. This term banner is a very ancient one. It is a derivative from band, a riband or ribbon worn by men of arms, sometimes on the helmet or head-piece, at others on some conspicuous portion of their garments. The color was that of the chief of the band. The word, as Noah Webster, the American Lexicographer, informs us, is substantially the same in the Saxon, the Swedish, the Danish, the Dutch, the German, the French, the English, the Spanish, the Portuguese, the Italian, the Irish, the Persian, and the Sanscrit languages.

In the 15th chapter of Numbers, verse 38th, the Israelites were commanded to wear a riband of blue on the borders of their garments, to look upon it, and remember God's commands, and to do them. That is, to remember that God was their leader, and that they were God's band or people.

In the time of Moses there does not appear to have been any National Banner among the Israelites. After the victory over Amalek, Moses set up a stone, engraved: *Jehovah-nissi.* "The Lord is my banner." Ex. xvii., ver. 15.

Each tribe of Israel, however, had its peculiar banner, probably of a color according with that of the stone in the breastplate of the high priest, inscribed with the name of the tribe, and emblazoned with devices symbolical of the blessing of Jacob to his sons respectively.

A banner was an ensign, depending from a staff, which could be carried by hand, usually by the chief of the band. Standards, as of the Assyrians, Egyptians, and other ancient peoples, were carried generally, if not always, on cars, or carriages, or ships. The bearer of a banner was usually called a banneret. In some of the Swiss cantons there was formerly a high officer, styled a banneret, who had charge of the banner of the canton. I think these earlier banners had an indent on the edge, opposite to the staff, or else terminated in a point. For bannerets, that is, feudal lords, who led their vassals to battle under their own banner, on the day of battle, and on the field of battle, after a victory, deeming themselves entitled to special commendation, presented their flags to the king or general, who cut off the train or skirt, and square. They were then called *knights of the squa* These square flags were called banners.

From the time of the first crusade, A. D. 1096, Christian nations a cross took the place of a riband Thus the Scots were distinguished by the Cross of drew. The banner of St. Andrew was a square flag bearing in white the Saltire of St. Andrew. This, t upon which St. Andrew was crucified, was represent white cross, corresponding to the diagonals of this The French were distinguished by a white cross, Italians by a blue one. The Spaniards bore a red cr the third crusade, A. D. 1188, the red cross of the S was appropriated by the French. The Flemish used cross, and the English a white one. This white cr used by the English until, having been assumed by herents of Simon Montfort, the rebellious Earl of L who fell in the battle of Eversham, August 4, A. l the National Cognizance was made the badge of a After this the Cross of St. George appears to ha adopted. At least it has been the badge of the l England and of the nation since the time of Edward D. 1327. It still adorns the National Flag of Great Parker, in his " Terms used in British Heraldry," say banner is a square flag, painted or embroidered wit and of a size proportioned to the rank of the bearer banner of St. George is white, charged with a re This red cross is not composed of the diagonals of the as in the case of the banner of St. Andrew, but of tw crossing each other at right angles ; one vertical, tl horizontal, intersecting at the middle of the square.

All the crosses given to the Crusaders were the cr the patron Saint of the nation, assigned to them by of the Church, the Pope of Rome. Their particu was doubtless worn by the men of each nation on t or surcoat, anciently called a jacquit or jacket. In t nances of Richard II., on the invasion of Scotlan

1386, and later by Henry V., it was directed "that every man, of what estate, condition, or nation they be of, so that they be of our party, bear the sign of the Arms of St. George, large, both before and behind, upon peril that if he be slayne or wounded to death, he that hath done so to him shall not be put to death, for default of the cross that he lacketh. And that none enemy do bear the same token or cross of St. George, notwithstanding if he be prisoner, upon pain of death." From this surcoat or jacket, flags, bearing such devices, are called Jacks. The Union of the Crosses of St. George and St. Andrew, since the Union of England and Scotland, 1707; and since 1808, the Union of the Crosses of St. George, St. Andrew, and St. Patrick, on the Union of England, Scotland, and Ireland, or, more properly speaking, Great Britain and Ireland, are called by the British Union Jacks. Nay, even the *Union* of our flag, the blue with the simple stars in place of the crosses is, by our naval men, called the U. S. Union Jack. So the banner of St. George is called the St. George's Jack, and the banner of St. Andrew the St. Andrew's Jack; and finally, among our Anglo-Saxon speaking nations, especially among naval and seafaring men, sailors themselves are called *Jack* Tars. At the risk of tediousness, I must return once more to the banners of St. George and St. Andrew. When James VI. of Scotland became also James I. of England, A. D. 1603, his subjects of Scotland and England, or of North and South Britain, as they were called, had violent contentions as to which flag, the banner of St. Andrew or the banner of St. George, should take precedence—that is, be saluted by the other. King James issued his royal proclamation on this subject April 12, 1606.

He ordered that both the ships of North Britain and South Britain should "bear in their main-top the red cross, commonly called St. George's cross, and the white cross, commonly called St. Andrew's cross, joined together, according to a form made by his heralds; and in their fore-top our subjects of South Britain shall wear the red cross only as they were wont, and the subjects of North Britain in their fore-top

the white cross only as they were accustomed." Ja
thoroughly a Scot. Therefore, the flag of Scotland w
the basis of this *new* flag, prepared by his heralds.
accordance with the rules of Heraldry, and doubtles
deference to the jealousy of his subjects of England, c
Britain, for their Red Cross Flag, which for centu
braved the battle and the breeze, the red cross alone
inserted in the banner of St. Andrew, but the red cr
a distinct margin of white about it, to show the banr
which it came, that of " Saynte George, whych ha
arms with a red cross. This blessed and holy Ma
George is patron of ye realme of England and ye cry€
of warre." This union of the banners of St. Andrew
George was called " *the king's colours.*" During the
the rival houses of York and Lancaster in England, 1
Cross Flag was for a time superseded by the red ar
roses, but was afterwards resumed as the flag of Engl

During the struggle between Charles I. and the Pa
of England, Charles set up the Royal Standard, emł
with the richest quarterings, the Lion, the Unicc
Roses, the Fleur de Luce, and the Thistle, etc. ; the
ment displayed the Red Cross Banner of St. Geo:
Merrie England. During the same struggle the Æ
Scotland, under Leslie, the disciple of Gustavus A(
had in their blue bonnets a bunch of blue ribands.
flag was blue, with the arms of Scotland embroiderec
upon it, and the motto : " For Christ's Crown and Co·

The " blue riband "of the Covenanters, and " the
of the hair" of the Puritans, were no doubt adopł
former from Numbers xv., ver. 38, and the latter from
xlvi., ver. 20—as emblems of God's chosen people.
mentions, Vol. II., p. 304, that the terms " Round
and " Cavaliers " came into vogue about the end (
The latter gave the rabble the appellation " Round
on account of the short cropped hair which they wor
called the others " Cavaliers." At what time precis€
blue riband " was adopted as the emblem of the Pro

I am not advised. In Miller's continuation of Hume, Vol. IV., p. 254, it is stated, that in 1780, when Lord Gordon presented a petition to Parliament against the extension of certain privileges to the Romanists, the procession was headed by the Protestant Association, and made up of 50,000 men, wearing the blue cockade. They compelled the members of the House of Commons to wear " the blue cockade " in passing to and from the House. There is no doubt Leslie brought the buff and blue, or blue and yellow uniform from the army of Gustavus Adolphus of Sweden, the Protector of the Protestants of his time, and they became the Whig colors. Hume, Vol. II., p. 575, says the names Whig and Tory were adopted about 1680, after the battle of Bothwell's Bridge. The former term is of Scottish, and the latter of Irish origin. In Sir Walter Scott's Legends of Montrose, Vol. XV., p. 33, ed. 1848, he puts into the mouth of Major Dugald Dalgetty, the soldier of fortune, when made by Montrose a Major of the Irish Brigade : " The Irish are pretty fellows—very pretty fellows. I desire to see none better in the field. I once saw a brigade of Irish at the taking of Frankfort on the Oder stand to it with sword and pike, until they beat off the blue and yellow Swedish brigades, esteemed as stout as any that fought under the immortal Gustavus." In I. F. Hollings' Life of Gustavus Adolphus, surnamed the Great, of Sweden, p. 106, it is mentioned Gustavus Adolphus first substituted the buff coat, as it was called, for the cuirass worn by Cavaliers. He made light artillery, carrying a four-pounds ball, of a copper tube, re-inforced at the breach with iron bands, all encased in boiled leather, which, when shrunk and hardened, was handsomely gilded and ornamented. He changed the formation of troops into lines instead of solid columns. He introduced the musket of a light pattern, which could be fired without a rest. He also armed his horsemen with a short musket. He caused different brigades to be distinguished by different colors. The Swedish brigades of blue and yellow were composed of Scots. Colonel Monro, who wrote the First and Second Expeditions, was the original of

Sir Walter Scott's Major Dugald Dalgetty. In another of his voluminous works, he mentions that the Flag of the Solemn League and Covenant, which England and Scotland entered into, A. D. 1643, was a Red Flag, with a blue border, and the motto, " For Christ's Crown and Covenant." The same statement is made in Howie's Scotch Worthies. I am credibly informed by an eminent Presbyterian divine that the Scotch Clergy of the Covenant wore blue garments instead of the ordinary clerical garb of black. In an old song on the battle of Bothwell's Bridge, June 22, 1679, occur the following lines about the Covenanters' flag. Scottish Ballads and Songs, James Maedment, Vol. II., p. 301 :

> " When he set up the flag o' red
> A' set about wi' bonnie blue,
> ' Since ye'll no cease and be at peace,
> See that ye stand by either true.' "

The last two lines are a quotation, and doubtless refer to the words of the motto, " For Christ's Crown and Covenant." Sir Walter Scott also mentions that the matchlock men of Leslie's army, who wore buff coats, had the bandoliers or shoulder belts, by which the spanners or wrenches of their matchlocks were suspended, of *blue*.

So the old nursery ballad :—

> "Oh dear ! what can the matter be ?
> Dear ! dear ! what can the matter be ?
> Oh dear ! what can the matter be,
>   Johnny's so long at the fair ?
> He promised to bring me a bunch of blue ribbons
>   To tie up my bonny brown hair.
> He promised to bring me a basket of posies,
> A garland of lilies, a garland of roses ;
> A little straw hat to set off the *blue ribbons*
>   That tie up my bonny brown hair."

This ancient ballad is of unknown origin, though itself well known. I have been told it took its rise in England at about the same time that the Royalists in Aberdeen tied blue

ribands about the necks of their lap-dogs, and called them
" Covenanting Dogs." I mention these trifles, because at
the beginning of our Revolutionary struggle there were all
sorts of leagues and covenants, called "agreements," etc.,
among the colonists. The first Continental Congress, 1774,
adopted a non-importation, non-consumption, and non-ex-
portation agreement for all the Colonies. The "Quebec
Act," giving extensive privileges to the Romanists in Canada,
called forth essays, and the display of a Union flag on the
Liberty Pole in this city, bearing the mottoes, " George Rex
and the Liberties of America" on one side ; on the reverse,
" No Popery ; " this in 1775. At the same time, in the ununiformed army before Boston, General Washington published
a General Order, that as General-in-Chief he would be distinguished by a broad blue riband, which, so soon as the
army was uniformed, was replaced by a uniform of blue and
buff—the uniform of our General and General Staff officers
to the present day. I am no bigot ; but the nation is and
has been, though tolerant of all religions, always Protestant,
and has never lost sight of Luther's early advocacy of universal education. D'Aubigné's History of the Reformation,
Vol. III., pp. 174–5.

After Charles I. was beheaded, January 30, 1649, the Red
Cross Flag, or St. George's Banner, continued to be the National Flag of England. Under Cromwell, as Macaulay says,
it became so respected that Rome halted in her persecutions
of the "Shepherds in the hamlets of the Alps, who professed
a Protestantism older than that of Augsburg." Nay, more,
at a mere hint from the Lord Protector, the Pope was forced
to preach humanity and moderation to Popish Princes. For
a voice, which seldom threatened in vain, declared that unless
favor was shown to the people of God, the English guns
should be heard in the Castle of St. Angelo. Under Charles
II., 1660 to 1685, disgrace followed disgrace. The Dutch
fleet sailed up the Thames, and burned the ships of war at
Chatham. The roar of foreign guns was heard, for the first
and last time, by the citizens of London. Under Anne, how-

ever, for a while it again beamed in mid-day splendor; the Duke of Marlborough by land, and Sir Cloudesley Shovel and Sir George Byng by sea, being the standard-bearers: until May 1, 1707, on the Union of England and Scotland, the flag made for King James by his heralds, called "the King's Colours," became the National Flag of Great Britain. From that time to this, flags bearing these devices have been called "Union" Flags. It is generally known that a ship in distress at sea displays her flag Union down.

At this period we find the Colonies of New England in a great commotion about flags. At Salem, Massachusetts, in 1635, John Endicott cut the red cross out of the flag, regarding it as idolatrous. He was removed from the magistracy, and rebuked, among other reasons, because it was feared that the Parliament of England, which used the Red Cross Flag, should regard this as an act of rebellion. It was proposed to use the Red and White Roses. Finally, in the last month of 1635, it was decided to leave out the Cross in all of the flags. It was appointed the King's Arms should be put into the Flag of Castle Island, where was a King's Fort, and Boston to be the first company. But in the first month of 1636, a ship called the St. Patrick, belonging to Sir Thomas Wentworth, Viceroy of Ireland, arrived, and one Miller, the master's mate, declared they were all rebels and traitors, because they had not "the King's Colours" at the Fort. Miller was induced to subscribe an apology. However, in the fourth month, at the request of the captains of ten vessels then in port, it was declared that as the fort was kept as the King's Fort, it was lawful to spread "*the King's Colours*" at Castle Island when the ships passed by, with the protestation that as they, the Governor and Council, held the Cross in the Ensign idolatrous, they could not set it up in their Ensigns. There was much of political caution displayed in all this matter of the flags.

The death of Charles I. having occurred January 30, 1649, in 1651 the General Court of Massachusetts resolved that the old English colors—that is, the St. George's Banner, used by the

Parliament of England—being a necessary distinction between the English and other nations in all places of the world, should be advanced on the Castle upon all necessary occasions, until the Parliament should alter the same, which they much desired.   Hazard, Vol. I., p. 554.

In 1652 the Colony of Massachusetts coined silver money, shillings, six-pences and three-pences.   Except the very first issue, which was very rude, they bore a *Tree* in the centre, with a double ring and the inscription Massachusetts, within it, on the one side, and New England, with the year 1652, and the value of the piece on the reverse.   Governor Hutchinson says it *all* bore the year " 1652," when " there was no king in Israel."   Hutchinson was, no doubt, correct as to the money in current use.   There appears to have been a special coinage of silver two-penny pieces in 1662, *after* Charles II. had become king.   There is every reason to suppose it was coined for the special purpose of placating King Charles II.   The resolution of the General Court, given at length, Vol. VII., Mass. His. Collections, says nothing of shillings, six-pences, or three-pences—it specifies *two-pences*. They did not bear a tree, " but a sort of shrub, spreading like a thistle."   The resolution was passed in 1662.   In 1663 Sir Thomas Temple, as we learn from Bancroft, appeared as the advocate of the Massachusetts Colony.   As Cromwell's Governor of Arcadia, he had resided long in New England during the interregnum.   On his arrival in England, 1663, he was sent for by King Charles II., to talk about affairs in Massachusetts.   " The King discovered great warmth against that colony."   " Among other things, he said they had invaded the royal prerogative in coining money.   Sir Thomas, who was a real friend of the colony, told his majesty that the colonists had but little acquaintance with law, and that they thought it no crime to make money for their own use.   In the course of the conversation, Sir Thomas took some of the money out of his pocket, and presented it to the King.   On one side of the coin was a pine tree, of that kind which is thick and bushy at the top.   The King inquired what tree

that was. Sir Thomas, artfully taking hold of the circum-
stance, informed his majesty it was the Royal Oak. The
Massachusetts people, says he, did not dare put your majesty's
name on their coin, and so put the Oak, which preserved
your life." After the battle of Worcester, September 3,
1651, Charles hid himself in a polled oak, which "a sort of
shrub, spreading like a thistle," would much resemble. A
writer in the Mass. His. Collections, under the signature *Σ*,
says of the two-penny-pieces : "All of them, I presume, have
the year 1662," and adds in a note : "It may be the letters
N. E. were on some of the pieces, instead of the date. The
impression is not to be distinguished clearly, but sometimes
it resembles the letters more than the date." "At least," he
continues, "of six that have come to my knowledge, two only
are in this particular legible." Mass. His. Collections, Vol.
VII., p. 229.

By this implication of loyalty on the part of the Massachusetts Colony, "the King, who was put into a fit of good
humor, said they were a parcel of honest dogs, and was disposed to hear favorable things of them." There is no doubt
in my mind this special coinage of 1662, with its impression,
not of a tree, "but of a sort of shrub, spreading like a
thistle," with N. E. also apparently on some of them in place
of the date, and their being of "two-penny-pieces," the only
ones of this small value coined, was, by pre-arrangement with
Sir Thomas Temple, struck that he might palm off on King
Charles the subterfuge that the tree on the coin was the
Royal Oak, and that the invasion of the royal prerogative of
coining money had been only in the small matter of two-
penny-pieces for local circulation.

It has been supposed there was a Flag of New England,
with a blue field, a St. George's Cross, and a green Tree in
the upper canton of the St. George's cross. I have had a
drawing sent to me of such a Flag, said to have been found
in some old plate of Flags. I would remark *en passant* these
plates of Flags are often quite fanciful. The use of such a
Flag by New England would have been flying in the face of

Cromwell, and of the Parliament, and the colonists never lost
sight of the King's " coming to his own again," as the phrase
was.   Edmund Randolph, called the " Court Spy," in an
able report on the Colony of Massachusetts to the Privy
Council, said : " A Tree was put upon their coin as an apt
symbol of their progressive vigor."   A writer in Mass. His.
Collections, already cited, as if there was an unusual, as well
as usual, name for the coins bearing the Tree, says, " usually
called Pine Trees."   Noah Webster says the " Cedar Tree,"
so often used in Scripture as an emblem of God's people, was
a species of " Pinus ; " may not this have been the *Tree* on
the Pine Tree coins ?   The first seal of Plymouth Colony, the
colony founded on Plymouth Rock, bearing date 1620, bore
on its shield a cross, subdividing the shield into four parts, in
each of which a man is represented, kneeling in a wilderness
and offering a burning heart to God.   See frontispiece Plymouth Records.   Again, as emblems of being God's chosen
people, the colonists of Connecticut put upon their seal a *Vine*
for each town or church ; at least there are fifteen separate
grapevines, bearing fruit, and a hand of Providence extended
out of the clouds, bearing a scroll or riband, on which is the
motto, " Sustinet qui Transtulit."   Conn. His. Coll., Vol. I.,
p. 251.   This colony seal was subsequently changed to one
of three vines and the above motto, and is now in part retained in the Arms of the State of Connecticut by three vines,
with the motto modified into " Qui Transtulit Sustinet."   Of
the Colony of New Haven, all record of its seal is lost.   But
the officers were styled the " Seven Pillars," referring to the
seven pillars of the House of Wisdom, as described by Solo-
mon.

In Ezekiel, chap. xlvi., ver. 20, " Zadoc and his sons,"
having been faithful to the Lord, were directed to distinguish
them as chosen.   " They shall only poll their heads."   From
this the Round-heads or Puritans drew the Scriptural au-
thority for cutting off " Love Locks," as they were called.
These " love locks " were worn by the Cavaliers, and were
quite distinct from the locks sometimes worn by the fair sex,

and called " Suivez moi jeune homme," or
translate it, " follow me, Johnny." By the
Ezekiel, a special favorite with the Puritans,
of those times very plainly show, the vine is
as the emblem of God's people. But the (
the close of chapter xvii. does it not say, '
would take of the highest branch of the high
one, and will plant it in a high mountain ar
the mountain of the height of Israel will I plai
bring forth boughs and bear fruit, and be a
and under it shall dwell all fowl of every wi
Hutchinson says of the date " 1652 " on the
tree, " when there was no king in Israel." C
the coin of Massachusetts have been the Good
It is true, the first seal of the Colony of Massacl
Indian erect, with an arrow in his right hand,
was the words in the vision of St. Paul : "
help us " (Bancroft, Vol. II., p. 347) to p
kingdom among the heathen. There is one c
coincidence. I mention it merely as such,
return from these flights of fancy to the dry
flag. In Ezekiel the emblems of supreme
Great Eagles. Is it not a remarkable coinc
chief bearing of the arms of our country is
Strong winged, but not full of feathers, fo
Eagle," to represent America. In his right
an olive branch, and in his left a bundle of ar
of the little " Democracie," planted on Rh
" a sheafe of arrows," with the motto, " Amor
Bancroft, Vol. I., p. 393.

The Flag in New England which next chal
was the Flag of Sir William Pepperell, und
burg, Cape Breton, was captured on the 17th
For this expedition " George Whitefield,"
preacher of those times, gave a motto for t
the proclamation of Queen Anne, 1707, necess
Flag. The motto was " Nil desperandum

This gave to the expedition the character of a crusade, and many of Whitefield's followers enlisted. One of them, a chaplain, carried on his shoulders a hatchet, with which he intended to destroy the images in the French churches. Belknap's New Hampshire, Vol. II., p. 204, 1791. We learn from Frothingham's Siege of Boston that "Union" Flags with mottoes were constantly displayed, at the time of the Colonies taking up arms, on Liberty Poles and Liberty Trees. At Concord and Lexington, as also at the battle of Bunker's Hill (I use the name by which it is commonly designated), fought June 17, 1775, just thirty years after the capture of Louisburg, Cape Breton, under Sir William Pepperell and Admiral Warren of the British Navy, I am satisfied there were no flags used except such as belonged to regiments or the companies of minute men. July 18, 1775, evidently to supply such a want, General Putnam displayed on Prospect Hill, before Boston, a red flag, with the mottoes, "Qui Transtulit Sustinet" and "Appeal to Heaven," in letters of gold. It is described by the master of an English transport to his owners as entirely red. The most authentic account gives the mottoes recited above. No doubt this Flag was sent to General Putnam from Connecticut. As in April, 1775, they fixed upon their standards and drums, the Colony Arms, and the motto "Qui Transtulit Sustinet ; " and as Massachusetts at the same time used the Flag, bearing a tree, with the motto, "Appeal to Heaven," it is more than probable this Flag bore those devices as well as the mottoes in gold. At a short distance Red and Gold or Orange would appear entirely red. Red and Orange are contiguous colors in the solar spectrum. The Red predominates over the Orange in the ratio of 45 to 27° measurement on the circumference of a circle. Hooker's Nat. Philosophy, p. 281.

September 13, 1775, when Colonel Moultrie received an order from the South Carolina Council of Safety for the taking of Fort Johnston, on James' Island, he had a large blue Flag made, with a crescent in one corner, to be in uniform with the troops. When the Turks took Constantinople, they found the crescent everywhere displayed on the churches and other buildings ; and regarding it as a good omen, they adopted it as their cognizance. October 20, 1775, we are informed, the Flag of the floating batteries, before Boston, was a Flag with a white ground, a tree in the middle, and the motto, " Appeal to Heaven."

In 1775, without organization, without uniforms, without any National Ensign, in fact, before there was a Union of all the Colonies, much was done. April 19, the first blood was shed at Lexington, and on the same day Captain Isaac Davis and others at Concord gave up their lives for the liberties of their country. May 10, 1775, Ethan Allen took by surprise Ticonderoga, and Seth Warner did the same as to Crown Point ; thus the command of Lake Champlain was secured, as well as cannon and ammunition for the army before Boston. General Washington was chosen, June 15, General to command all the Continental forces. June 17, the battle of Bunker's Hill was fought, and General Warren fell. July 2, General Washington arrived at Cambridge. In General Orders, issued by him July 14, 23, and 24, badges were ordered, as the first step in discipline in the ununiformed army. His own badge, as I have already stated, was a broad blue riband, worn upon his breast, between his coat and waistcoat. This has often been imagined to be the baldric of a Marshal of France. He never was a Marshal of France. This army was in want of everything. August 12, the Provincial Congress of Massachusetts agreed upon recommending it to the inhabitants, the scarcity of ammunition being so alarming, not to fire a gun at beast, bird, or mark, without real necessity. Notwithstanding all these drawbacks, an expedition was fitted out under Arnold, by the way of Kennebec, against Quebec, while another under Montgomery moved down Lake Champlain with the same object. A similar spirit was manifested everywhere. October 18, Chamblay surrendered to Majors Brown and Livingston. Among the trophies were the colors of the 7th Regiment, doubtless Royal Fusileers ; these were the first captured colors ever

2

presented to Congress. Gordon Amer. Rev., Vol. I., p. 426. The attack on Quebec failed, and Montgomery fell, December 31, 1775.

January 2, 1776, the Great Union Flag of the Colonies, a "Union" Flag of 1707, already described, with thirteen stripes, alternate red and white for the field, was substituted for the Flag displayed by General Putnam, July 18, 1775, on Prospect Hill. This Great Union Flag was displayed on the day the new army about Boston was formed, in compliment to the thirteen United Colonies. The King's proclamation had been sent out of Boston by a flag of truce, January 1, 1776. General Washington wrote the display of this Flag, January 2, 1776, "farcically enough," was taken as a signal of surrender. Lieut. Carter, a British officer, explains "the reason why" by stating that it was taken for two distinct flags—"the British Union" above the "Continental Union of thirteen stripes." Whereas, being the Flag of British Colonies in arms to secure the rights and liberties of British subjects, it was a British Union Flag, with a field of thirteen stripes, alternate red and white. In plate vii. of Preble's History of the American flag, a *fac-simile* of the Flag of the schooner Royal Savage, a Continental Union Flag, as described above, is given. The drawing was made in 1776. It was found by Benson J. Lossing, a most diligent and painstaking collector of invaluable details connected with our country's history, among the papers of Major-General Philip Schuyler. This Continental Union Flag, on the evacuation of Boston by the British, and its occupation by the troops of the United Colonies, was carried by Ensign Richards, General Putnam being in command of the forces which took possession of the forts, etc., from which the British retreated, March 18, 1776. This was *the American Flag* saluted at St. Eustatius by the Dutch, by order of the Governor, Johannes De Graef, November 16, 1776,[1] as it was displayed from the peak of the brigantine Andrew Doria, com-

---

[1] See article, New York *Times*, Sunday, January 21, 1877.

manded by Captain Nicholas Biddle, one of the first vessels procured for the Navy of the United Colonies. It was what was called the *Continental Union Flag.* The stars and stripes did not become the Flag of the United States until June 14, 1777; consequently could not have been saluted as such November 16, 1776.

In the meantime, Admiral Hopkins sailed from the Capes of the Delaware, February 17, 1776. Paul Jones was senior First Lieutenant of the fleet, and raised the Continental Union Flag, displayed by the army before Boston, January 2, 1776, and " the Standard of the Commander-in-Chief of the American Navy," as described in the records of the South Carolina Provincial Congress, February 9, 1776, to whom Colonel Gadsden, Chairman of the Committee on Naval Affairs, presented it, " being a yellow field, with a lively representation of a rattlesnake in the middle, in the attitude of striking, with the words underneath, ' Don't tread on me ' " (American Archives, 4th Series, Vol. V., p. 568), on the Alfred, Captain Dudley Saltonstall, on which ship Admiral Hopkins spread his broad pennant. The colors of his fleet were thus described in a letter, dated New Providence (West Indies), May 13, 1776 : " The colours of the American fleet were striped under the *Union* with thirteen strokes, called the United Colonies, and their standard, a rattlesnake ; motto, ' Don't tread on me.' J. Carson Brevoort, who is in possession of the Log of Paul Jones when he commanded the squadron composed of his flagship, the " Bonne Homme Richard," the Alliance, Captain Landais, etc., has kindly furnished me with a drawing of the flag of Commodore Paul Jones, as he is called by the Dutch Admiral at the Texel. It had no rattlesnake on it. It was, however, somewhat curious, as was that of Captain Landais. After capturing the Serapis, September 23, 1779, Paul Jones was obliged to pass on board his prize. The Dutch authorities at the Texel were at a loss as to his nationality. By the usage of Great Britain the first flag is the Royal Standard ; the second, the Anchor of Hope, Flag of the Lord High Admiral ;.

third, the Great Union throughout, Flag of the Admiral of the fleet ; fourth, Great Union with a red field, Admiral's flag ; fifth, Great Union, with a white field, Vice-Admiral's flag ; sixth, Great Union, with a blue field, Rear Admiral's flag. Hence the names Admiral of the Red, Admiral of the White, and Admiral of the Blue.

Jones and Landais had a quarrel about precedence. Jones undoubtedly regarded himself as an Admiral of the Blue, for his commission, by especial provision, was that of Commander-in-Chief of the fleet ; for his flag was a blue Union, with thirteen stars of eight points each, four stars in the topmost row, five stars in the middle row, and four in the bottom row. The topmost stripe of the field was blue, the second red, the third white, the fourth red, the fifth white, the sixth blue, the seventh red, the eighth white, the ninth red, the tenth blue, the eleventh white, the twelfth blue, the thirteenth red. In the official records of Texel this Flag is thus described : " Noord Americaansche Vlag, Van d'Serapis en genomme Engels Oor logs Fregatt thaus gecommandeerd door den Noord Americaansche Commandant Paul Jones, sord Texel binnen gekomen den 5 October, 1779." While at the Texel " Commodore Paul Jones" was invited in writing, by Vice-Admiral Réyun of the Dutch Navy, to admit that, though he sailed under a commission from the United States, it was no less true he also had a commission from France. Paul Jones' reply is so characteristic, I give it from the original in possession of Mr. Brevoort. It was endorsed, or rather written below the communication from Vice-Admiral Réyun. It is in the following words, viz. :

" N. B. The above is the proposition that was given me in writing, the 13th of December, 1779, on board the Alliance, at Texel, by M. le Chev⁣ᵣ de Lironcourt, to induce me to say and sign a Falsehood.

" (Signed)   PAUL JONES."

Landais' flag, as recorded by the same authorities at the Texel, may be thus described : possibly he modified his flag to be that of an Admiral of the White, the next grade above the Admiral of the Blue; or else desired to compliment France, the Flag of which had a white ground. Union blue —thirteen stars of eight points. 1st, row of stars, three stars; 2d, two stars; 3d, three stars; 4th, two stars; 5th, three stars. Field of Flag—Topmost row, white; 2d, red; 3d, white; 4th, red; 5th, white; 6th, red; 7th, white; 8th, red; 9th, white; 10th, red; 11th, white; 12th, red; 13th, white. Noord Americaansche Vlag. Van d' L'Alliance ge commandeered door Captain Landais In Texel binnen gekomen den 4th October, 1779.

It is possible Paul Jones used the Rattlesnake Standard, already described, but I find no evidence of the fact. The only public instrument in use retaining some record of the part the " rattlesnake " bore in our flag, and on the drums of the Marine Corps, is the seal in the War Department. It bears the rattlesnake, with its rattles, as the emblem of union, and a liberty cap in contiguity with the rattles; the liberty cap enveloped by the body, so that the opened mouth may defend the rattles and liberty cap, or union and liberty, with the motto, '' This we'll defend.''

June 7, 1776, Richard Henry Lee introduced the resolution, '' that the United Colonies are and ought to be free and independent States.'' It was unanimously adopted July 2, 1776. July 4, 1776, the Declaration of Independence, penned by Thomas Jefferson, was adopted. On the same day Dr. Franklin, Mr. J. Adams and Mr. Jefferson were appointed a committee to prepare a device for a Great Seal for the United States of America.

August 10, 1776, this committee reported as follows: '' The Great Seal should on one side have the Arms of the United States of America, which arms should be as follows: The Shield has six quarters, parts one, *Coupé* two. The 1st or, a rose, enamelled gules and argent for England; the 2d, argent, a thistle proper, for Scotland; the 3d verd, a harp or, for Ireland; the 4th azure, a *flower de luce* or, for France; the 5th or, the imperial eagle, sable for Germany; and 6th or, the Belgic lion, gules for Holland, pointing out the countries from which the States have been peopled. The shield within a border gules entwined of thirteen Scutcheons argent, linked together by a chain or, each charged with initial letters sable as follows : 1st, N. H. ; 2d, M. B. ; 3d, R. I. ; 4th, C. ; 5th, N. Y. ; 6th, N. J. ; 7th, P. ; 8th, D. E. ; 9th, M. ; 10th, V. ; 11th, N. C. ; 12th, S. C. ; 13th, G. ; for each of the thirteen independent States of America. Supporters ; dexter, the Goddess Liberty, in a corselet of armor, alluding to the present times ; holding in her right hand the spear and cap, and with her left supporting the shield of the States ; sinister, the Goddess Justice, bearing a sword in her right hand, and in her left a balance. Crest. The eye of Providence in a radiant triangle ; whose glory extends over the shield and beyond the figures. Motto : *E Pluribus Unum.* Legend round the whole achievement—Seal of the United States of America, MDCCLXXVI. On the other side of the said Great Seal should be the following device : Pharaoh sitting in an open chariot, a crown on his head and a sword in his hand, passing through the divided waters of the Red Sea in pursuit of the Israelites. Rays from a pillar of fire in the cloud, expressive of the divine presence and command, beaming on Moses, who stands on the shore, and extending his hand over the sea, causes it to overthrow Pharaoh. Motto : 'Rebellion to tyrants is obedience to God.' "

It was ordered to lay on the table.

The closing words, " Rebellion to tyrants is obedience to God," are from the epitaph of John Bradshaw, chief of the regicides. They are written over what is called the Regicides' Cave, West Rock, New Haven, Conn. Mr. Hollis, in his memoirs, mentions that he found the epitaphs at length, pasted up on the windows of inns in New England, in the early days of our Revolutionary struggle, and states the fact as an evidence of the spirit which actuated our forefathers.

The original of the following is engraven upon a cannon, at the summit of a steep hill, near Martha Bray, in Jamaica (see

Memoirs of Mr. Hollis, Vol. II., p. 789), reprinted in Gentleman's Magazine, XIV., 834 :

" Stranger,
Ere thou pass, contemplate this cannon.
Nor regardless be told
That near its base lies deposited the dust
Of JOHN BRADSHAW ;
Who, nobly superior to selfish regards,
Despising alike the pageantry of courtly
splendour,
The blast of calumny,
And the terrors of royal vengeance,
Presided in the illustrious band
of Heroes and Patriots,
Who fairly and openly adjudged
CHARLES STUARD,
Tyrant of England,
To a public and exemplary death ;
Thereby presenting to the amazed world,
And transmitting down through applauding ages,
The most glorious example
Of unshaken virtue,
Love of Freedom,
And impartial Justice,
Ever exhibited on the blood-stained theatre
Of human actions.
Oh, Reader, pass not on,
Till thou hast blest his memory,
And never, never forget,
That REBELLION TO TYRANTS
IS OBEDIENCE TO GOD."

Cornwallis surrendered at Yorktown, Va., October 19, 1781. The country remained without any Great Seal until June 20, 1782.

The " Continental Union Flag," displayed January 2, 1776, as before stated, continued to be used until June 14, 1777, just one hundred years ago, when the Congress " Resolved, That the Flag of the Thirteen United States be thirteen stripes, alternate red and white. That the Union be thirteen stars, white in a blue field, representing a new constellation." Paul Jones, in command of the Ranger, demanded and received from the French Admiral in Quiberon Bay, coast of

Brittany, the first salute to the Stars and Stripes, as adopted June 14, 1777, *Gun* for *Gun.*

It had been before that event the usage of Europe to salute the Flag of a Republic with four guns less than were fired to salute the Flag of a crowned potentate.

It will be observed no form for the presentation of the stars, in any particular shape, was defined by the resolution ; consequently various forms were adopted. Because the circle is the simplest of all figures, and for the reasons following, I suppose them at first to have been arranged in a circle.

John Adams—the father of J. Q. Adams—was Chairman of the Board of War when the resolution of June 14, 1777, was passed, and also, as has been stated, one of the Committee appointed July 3, 1776, to prepare a Great Seal for the United States. When eleven years of age, J. Q. Adams crossed the Atlantic with his father under this flag. After having been Secretary of Legation to the United States Minister to Russia, at the age of fifteen, Mr. J. Q. Adams came from England, where he had represented the United States at the Court of St. James, to become Secretary of State of the United States, under the administration of President Monroe. This in 1817. All citizens, especially youthful ones in a foreign land, look to the flag of their country with feelings and an interest quite different from citizens at home. Mr. J. Q. Adams must have been curious about it when he sailed under its folds at the age of eleven. As Secretary of Legation, at the age of fifteen, he could not readily have lost sight of it. As Minister, it was the ensign of his country among a proud and supercilious people. When he returned, to become Secretary of State, a change in it was being discussed in Congress. In the annals of Congress, 2d Session, 1816–1817, the discussion will be found at large. It was deemed inexpedient to alter the flag. Many thought it should have been always retained as resolved upon June 14, 1777. However, December 11, 1817, Mr. Wendover, of New York, an owner of many ships, moved the following :

" Resolved, That a committee be appointed to inquire into

the expediency of altering the Flag of the United States, and that they have leave to report by bill or otherwise." Mr. Wendover remarked : " Had the flag of the United States never have undergone an alteration, he certainly should not, he said, propose to make a further alteration. It was his impression, and he thought it was generally believed, that the flag would be essentially injured by an alteration, on the same principles as that which had been made by increasing the stripes and stars. He stated the incongruity of the flag in general use, and instanced the flag flying over the building in which Congress sat, and that of the navy yard, one of which contained *nine* stripes, and the other *eighteen ;* neither of them conformable to law. It was of some importance, he conceived, that the flag of the nation should be designated with precision, and that the practice under the law should be conformed to its requirements." The motion was agreed to without opposition. Annals of Congress, 1st Session, Vol. I., 1817–1818, p. 463.

When the Committee reported, there was a protracted discussion, which may be found in the same volume, page 567, and volume ii., page 1463. Finally, the resolution, approved April 4, 1818, was passed March 25, 1818. Mr. Wendover suggested that at the rate the Union was growing, if a stripe was added for every new State admitted, it would soon be impracticable to find a mast tall enough on which to hoist the flag. This practical suggestion determined the action of Congress.

During the time of this discussion, Mr. J. Q. Adams was Secretary of State. The original flag, so far as the stripes were concerned, was reverted to by the resolution of April 4, 1818. The only departure from it was that, instead of *thirteen* stars in the Union of the flag, a star was to be introduced into that Union for each new State on the 4th of July succeeding the admission of such State to the Union of the United States. But in 1819 the angry discussion about the bill authorizing the people of the territory of Missouri to form a Constitution and State Government for admission into the Union began. Hon. Henry Clay, by his compromise meas-

ures, brought relief to the country.   The Enabling Act was
passed and approved by President Monroe, March 6, 1820.
August 25, 1820, Mr. J. Q. Adams, Secretary of State when
the alteration of the flag to suit the growth of the nation was
discussed, Secretary of State also when the Union was
threatened, on account of the Enabling Act for Missouri,
struck from the United States Passport the National Arms,
as declared by Act of Congress, and substituted the figure
and device of an Eagle, holding in his beak the constellation
Lyra, of thirteen stars, a glory radiating from Lyra into a
circle of thirteen stars, and the motto, " Nunc Sidera Ducit."
This seal Mr. J. Q. Adams had caused to be engraved in
England before 1817.   It is now in the possession of his son,
Hon. Charles Francis Adams.   The last-named gentleman is
of opinion Mr. John Adams had nothing to do with suggest-
ing the constellation Lyra.   Perhaps it never was suggested
for the Union of the Flag.   If it was not, what could have
warranted so great a departure from the universal practice of
nations as the substitution of a fanciful device for the arms of
the nation on a document intended everywhere to establish
the nationality of the citizen provided with it, and this substitution with the consent and approval of the President of
the United States, were it not the desire to make some en-
during record of the origin of the thirteen stars in the Union
of the first Flag of the United States in the constellation of
the Lyre of Orpheus ?   In this device the thirteen stars are
in a *circle*.   In the same form they are represented on the
copper coins of 1783, and on some of the Continental paper
money, with the words, " Nova Constellatio," " A new Constellation ; " and, finally, on a representation of the first Flag
of the United States, in a drawing to accompany a project
for the Arms of the United States, now on file in the Department of State, the thirteen stars are arranged in a *circle*.
This, however, is merely an hypothesis, more curious perhaps than important.*

---

* The words within brackets were not part of the address as delivered before
the N. Y. Historical Society.   They are added to make the paper complete.

Fig. 1.

Fig. 3.

Fig. 2.

[The thirteen stars, white in a blue field, representing a new constellation, were frequently displayed, as shown in Fig. 1 herewith, on maps, pictures, etc., notably Bauman's map of siege of Yorktown, Va., October, 1781, in possession of N. Y. Historical Society.

Fig. 3 represents the flag raised before Boston, January 2, 1776. It was simply the British Union of the Crosses of St. George and St. Andrew on a blue field for the union, and a field of thirteen stripes alternate red and white for the field of the flag.

Fig. 2 shows the disposition of the stars in Fig. 1 was simply disposing the thirteen stars in the union of the flag so as to preserve a trace of the crosses of St. George and St. Andrew, the thirteen stars supplanted in that Union. The dotted lines in Fig. 2 show the crosses of St. George and St. Andrew with the stars disposed as in Fig. 1. This could not have been a mere accident. Even in those early days the people were unwilling to give up *their old flag*, and thus preserved a reminiscence of it, though Congress fixed no form for the display of the thirteen stars in the Union of the flag.

In 1861, our misguided fellow-citizens of the South made a capital mistake, practically and politically, by *not* firing on the OLD FLAG at Fort Sumter from under the OLD FLAG. By so doing they would have taken the pith and marrow out of the songs of the people—" Rally round the flag, boys," " The red, white, and blue," etc. Washington and his compeers were content to fight at first under the " British Union " distinguished by thirteen stripes or ribands, alternate red and white in the field of the flag. Stripes or ribands of different colors, as heretofore stated, were the insignia of rank in the uniformed army before Boston, from Gen. Washington down. These stripes or ribands, heraldry warranting it, naturally were embodied, in the " Great Union Flag of the United Colonies," in its field, as in our National Flag to-day.

No doubt the disposition of the thirteen stars, as shown in Fig. 1, was the origin of the practice of placing the stars, now so numerous, in rows or ribands. This was a happy,

though doubtless unintentional, mode of perpetuating "the
wearing of the ribands" as a badge of distinction by Washington and his brethren in arms in the army before Boston,
prior to January 2, 1776, when flag Fig. 3 was first displayed,
the field of which was thirteen red and white ribands. In the
flag which supplanted it January 14, 1777, not only in the
ribands of the field, but also in the stars of its union, under
the form given Fig. 1, the reminiscence of the British crosses
was preserved, and also "the wearing of the ribands." On
the other hand, the circle signified perpetuity, and after all
so does the cross and parallel lines only meet in infinity.
So there is perpetuity under all the forms.]

I revert now to the struggles in the Colonies. While these
were going on there was as yet only a silent growth, no
marked fruit of intellectual development, if I except Jonathan
Edwards' renowned work on Free Will. He died President
of the College of New Jersey, now Princeton College, 1758.

I cannot attempt, for space will not admit of it, and they
may be found in almost any school history, all the victories
by sea and land won under this Flag of Thirteen Stars and
Thirteen Stripes. I may not omit the names of Washington,
Schuyler, Stark, whose Mary was to be a widow if they did
not beat the Hessians by set of sun at Bennington; of stout
old General Herkimer, who gave his life for the cause; Ma-
rion, Sumpter, Huger, Light Horse Harry Lee, Benjamin
Lincoln, who replied to Washington, on the latter expressing
his surprise that the Northern people, with nothing but their
rocks and brains, should be willing to fight for liberty, "We
fight for liberty to use our brains," and to another, who ex-
pressed some fear, "Fear nothing, sir," said this brave old
soldier, "fear nothing but sin;" Morgan and his famous
riflemen; Green, whose Fabian caution redeemed the disasters of Gates; Knox, Pickering, Hamilton, Hugh Mercer,
who fell, covered with wounds, at Princeton, January 3, 1777,
of which he died January 19, 1777; Wayne, called Mad Anthony, the hero of the storming of Stony Point on the Hud-
son; De Kalb, Steuben, Kosciusko, Pulaski, mortally

wounded before Savannah, October 6, 1779, Lafayette, and a host of others; and last, but not least, the determined Colonel Peter Gansevoort, who, when beleaguered by St. Leger at Fort Stanwix, since Fort Schuyler, now the city of Rome, Oneida County, New York, replied to St. Leger's demand for the surrender of the fort, August 9, 1776: "It is my determined resolution, with the force under my command, to defend this fort to the last extremity, in behalf of the United States, who have placed me here to defend it against all their enemies." Here no doubt was first displayed in battle the stars and stripes. Colonel Marinus Willett, Lieut.-Colonel Mellon, and Captain Abraham Swartwout, of Dutchess County, were the brave official coadjutors of Colonel, afterwards General Gansevoort. The blue of the Union of the flag was made out of Captain Swartwout's cloak, the white stars and stripes out of pieces of shirt, sewed together, and bits of scarlet cloth for the red. Lossing, Vol. I., p. 242. My aged grandmother, a daughter of Major-General Philip Schuyler, informed me the red stripes were furnished by the scarlet cloak of one of the women of the beleaguered garrison. Such cloaks were much worn at that time in this country. Benedict Arnold here, as at other times, rendered brilliant services to his country. One is almost tempted to drop a tear over the noble beginning, which had the fateful ending of an exiled traitor's grave. On the ocean, Manly, the father of the American Navy, began his career in the Lee. The names of Nicholson, Saltonstall, Biddle, Thompson, Barry, Reade, Jones, Wickes, etc., come before us. In 1776, 342 sail of English vessels were taken by American cruisers. In 1777, 467 sail were taken, and thus matters went on, with many brilliant conflicts of ship with ship. Fenimore Cooper's History of the U. S. Navy. Anthony Wayne, the hero of Stony Point, August 20, 1794, quelled the Indians at the Fallen Timbers, near the Maumee Rapids. The National Flag continued with thirteen stars and thirteen stripes, until the resolution approved January 13, 1794, when Congress enacted "that after May 1, 1795, the Flag of the United States be fifteen stripes, alternate red and white.   That the Union be fifteen stars, white in a blue field."

The thirteen original States ratified our present Constitution at the dates set opposite to them, respectively:

```
New Hampshire..........................June 21, 1788.
Massachusetts..........................February 6, 1788.
Rhode Island...........................May 29, 1790.
Connecticut............................January 9, 1788.
New York...............................July 26, 1788.
New Jersey.............................December 18, 1787.
Pennsylvania...........................December 12, 1787.
Delaware...............................December 7, 1787.
Maryland...............................April 28, 1788.
Virginia...............................June 26, 1788.
North Carolina.........................November 21, 1789.
South Carolina.........................May 23, 1788.
Georgia................................January 2, 1788.
```

Vermont had been admitted as a State, March 4, 1791.   In the same year Benjamin West was chosen President of the Royal Academy of Art, London.   Kentucky was admitted June 1, 1792.   In the meantime how much had been done! The Ordinance of 1787 for the government of the North-west Territory was passed.   A government of the people, by the people, and for the people had been framed and ratified. "The Federalist," as remarkable for the vigor, beauty, and purity of its style, as for its invaluable comments on our form of government, had been written by Madison, Jay, and Hamilton.   Of the latter Webster said: "He smote the rock of national resources, and abundant streams of revenue gushed forth.   He touched the dead corpse of the Public Credit, and it sprung upon its feet.   The fabled birth of Minerva, from the brain of Jove, was hardly more sudden or more perfect than the financial system of the United States, as it burst forth from the conceptions of Alexander Hamilton."   I trust I may be pardoned for this allusion to my illustrious grandsire.   The History of the Flag of our country would be incomplete without some notice of his eminent services.   In 1794 Whitney invented the cotton-gin.   Tennessee was admitted June 1, 1796. George Washington died December 14, 1799. In 1800 the National Capitol was removed from Philadelphia to Washington. Ohio was admitted November 29, 1802. In 1802 the United States Military Academy at West Point was established. Louisiana was purchased 1803. Between 1803 and 1805 our Navy, under Bainbridge, Morris, Preble, Decatur, Chauncey, Barron, Rogers, Porter, and the gallant Captain Somers, who was blown up (it was never known how, in the ketch Intrepid, off Tripoli), with all his company, rendered brilliant service. Of Captain Somers we are told : Commodore Preble having remarked, while trying a port-fire in the cabin of the Constitution, " He thought it burned longer than was necessary." Somers quietly rejoined, " I ask for no port-fire at all." These brave men and their comrades taught the Mohammedans of the Barbary States " that westward the course of Empire takes its way ;" that a Christian nation of the West, whose Flag even they did not know, to use Charles Cotesworth Pinckney's words on the occasion of our differences with France, had " Millions for defence, not one cent for tribute ;" and the enslaving of Christians by the followers of the Prophet ceased from June 8, 1805. The foreign slave-trade was abolished by our Federal Constitution, to take effect 1808. (See history of legislation on the subject of the slave-trade, in the charge of Justice Wayne, United States Supreme Court, to United States District Court, Savannah, Georgia, November, 1859.) The United States Coast Survey was inaugurated February 10, 1807. In the same year Robert Fulton built the first steamboat in the world for practical purposes. It was called the " North River." In the same year the " Leopard," a British man-of-war, impressed three Americans from the United States man-of-war " Chesapeake," which had gone to sea in an unprepared condition.

James Madison was inaugurated President, March 4, 1809. General William Henry Harrison, November 7, 1811, gained the battle of Tippecanoe. Louisiana was admitted to the Union, April 8, 1812. In this year war was declared against Great Britain. The suicidal policy of an embargo had been foolishly tried by the United States, almost destroying the feeble remains of our commerce and dividing the nation. After many disasters by land, the brilliant affair of Fort George, May 27, 1813, in which Lieutenant-Colonel Winfield Scott led the assault, took place. September 10, 1813, Oliver Hazard Perry, on Lake Erie, reported of his splendid success at Put-in Bay: "We have met the enemy, and they are ours." General Harrison defeated Proctor, October 5, 1813, at the Moravian Town on the Thames. Captain James Lawrence, of this city, in the "Chesapeake," whose original tombstone stands in the vestibule of the New York Historical Society, engaged the British man-of-war "Shannon," June 6, 1813. He lost his ship and his life—his last words were: "Don't give up the ship." General Andrew Jackson crushed the Creeks at Horse Shoe Bend, on the Tallapoosa River. Our Flag was still of fifteen stars and fifteen stripes. In 1814, July 5, under General Brown, at Chippewa, General Scott led a brilliant bayonet charge against the British, and a great success was achieved. July 25, 1814, the battle of Lundy's Lane was fought—rendered famous by Colonel Miller's laconic reply when asked could he storm a battery with his regiment, the Twenty-first United States Infantry: "I'll try," and did it. At this time West Point began to tell. Our fellow-citizen, Alexander McComb, Major-General United States Army, was Inspector of that institution. Joseph G. Swift, the first graduate, born in Massachusetts; Walker P. Armisted, Virginia; William McRee, North Carolina; Joseph G. Totten, Connecticut; Eleazer D. Wood, New York, rendered most distinguished services. On the 15th of August, 1814, under Major-General Edmund Pendleton Gaines, of Virginia, the British were repulsed from Fort Erie with great slaughter. Here George Mercer Brook, of Virginia, afterwards Major-General, won the sobriquet of the "Jack-a-Lanthorn of Fort Erie." September 11, 1814, Commodore McDonough won the brilliant and decisive victory of Lake Champlain. In the meantime, however, the

British burned all the public buildings at Washington, except the Patent Office and Post Office. They bombarded Baltimore, and inspired the "Star -Spangled Banner." January 8, 1815, General Jackson won the battle of New Orleans. Many brilliant combats were fought on the ocean. These combats were so numerous, that those interested must consult Cooper's History of the United States Navy. Indiana was admitted December 11, 1816 ; Mississippi, December 10, 1817. In the same year, through the efforts of De Witt Clinton, the Act authorizing the Erie Canal was passed in this State, and the canal was completed in 1825. April 4, 1818, the following resolution was adopted by Congress. Our National Flag up to this time had, since the Resolution of January 13, 1794, continued to be fifteen stripes, alternate red and white, the Union fifteen stars, white, in a blue field :

Be it enacted, etc., " That from and after the fourth of July next, the flag of the United States be thirteen horizontal stripes, alternate red and white ; that the Union be twenty stars, white, in a blue field."

" And, that on the admission of a new State into the Union, one star be added to the Union of the flag ; and that such addition shall take effect on the fourth of July next succeeding such admission. Approved April 4, 1818."

Illinois was admitted December 3, 1818. Alabama was admitted December 14, 1819. The steamship " Savannah," in this year, sailed from Savannah, Ga., for Liverpool, being twenty-six days on the passage. Thence to St. Petersburg, Russia, and arrived at Savannah fifty days from St. Petersburg, December 15, 1819. *Niles' Weekly Register*, September 18, 1819, and *Evening Gazette*, date ——, Signature W.

Maine was admitted March 15, 1820. Missouri, August 10, 1821. Arkansas, June 15, 1836. In the intervening period, 1831, the first locomotive in America was used on the Baltimore and Ohio Railroad, under the personal supervision of our venerated fellow-citizen, Peter Cooper. I quote many of my data from Venables' United States History, a valuable epitome. Michigan was admitted January 26, 1837.

In 1842, Professor S. F. B. Morse established telegraphic communication between Castle Garden, New York City, and Governor's Island; and in 1844 he set up the first electric telegraph in the world, for practical purposes, between Baltimore and Washington.

Florida was admitted March 3, 1845. In 1845 the U. S. Naval Academy was founded. It was recommended in 1798. We all know the valuable fruit it has already borne to our country and to our naval service. Texas, December 29, 1846. The country went on growing, and except the Indian wars—which have been chronic—at peace with all the world. Andrew Jackson, by his firmness, had nipped nullification in the bud. His "By the Eternal, the Union must and shall be preserved," saved the country from civil war. His was a voice like Cromwell's—it seldom threatened in vain. To General Scott he entrusted the execution of his orders at Charleston. Jackson knew him to be a true patriot.

The admission of Texas involved us in a war with Mexico. General Zachary Taylor, at Resaca de la Palma, Palo Alto, Monterey, and Buena Vista, sustained the glory of our flag against great odds. Let us pause for a moment, while I rehearse a verse or two of a song composed and sung by our soldiers after the victory of Palo Alto. They found in the caps of the dead Mexicans, who, poor fellows, fell fighting for their native land, a General Order of General Arista, urging his troops, who were poorly subsisted, to victory by the promise of abundance after they had captured the flour of the Americans. Our soldiers also had a notion the Mexicans used copper instead of leaden bullets. The copper supposed to be more deadly. The song was to the tune of "The Rose of Alabama." It had about 500 verses. Of these, I only remember two:

> "He said he would the Yankees take
> Their flour into bread he'd bake,
> But we knocked his pancakes into dough
> On the plains of Palo Alto.—CHORUS.

" We'll batter down his mudden walls,
    Make cymbals of his copper balls,
    And dance in Don Arista's halls,
    To the tune of Palo Alto."

We did it at Monterey, of which our fellow-citizen, Charles Fenno Hoffman, wrote the following lines ; I think them very beautiful :

" We were not many—we who stood
    Before the iron sleet that day ;
    Yet many a gallant spirit would
    Give half his years if but he could
    Have been with us at Monterey.

" Now here, now there, the shot it hailed
    In deadly drifts of fiery spray,
    Yet not a single soldier quailed
    When wounded comrades round them wailed
    Their dying shout at Monterey.

" And on—still on our column kept
    Through walls of flame its withering way ;
    Where fell the dead, the living stept,
    Still charging on the guns which swept
    The slippery streets of Monterey.

" The foe himself recoiled aghast,
    When, striking where he strongest lay,
    We swooped his flanking batteries past,
    And braving full their murderous blast,
    Stormed home the towers of Monterey.

" Our banners on those turrets wave,
    And there our evening bugles play ;
    Where orange boughs above their grave
    Keep green the memory of the brave,
    Who fought and fell at Monterey.

" We were not many—we who pressed
    Beside the brave who fell that day ;
    But who of us has not confessed
    He'd rather share their warrior rest
    Than not have been at Monterey ? "

Of the operations of General Scott—Vera Cruz, Cerro Gordo, Contreras, Churubusco, Molino del Rey, Chapulte-pec and the City of Mexico, over which our flag floated in triumph September 14, 1848, with thirty stars in its union (for Iowa had been admitted December 28, 1846), Sir Henry Bulwer, accredited Minister of Great Britain to the United States, Nov. 30, 1850, at the celebration of St. Andrew's day, in New York City, said : "If Waverley and Guy Mannering had made the name of Scott immortal on one side of the Atlantic, Cerro Gordo and Chapultepec had equally immortalized it on the other. If the novelist had given the garb of truth to fiction, had not the warrior given to truth the air of romance ? "—*National Intelligencer*, Dec. 4, 1850.

In his turn, General Scott said, in reference to the United States Military Academy, June 21, 1860 : "I give it as my fixed opinion that, but for our graduated cadets, the war between the United States and Mexico might, and probably would, have lasted some four or five years, with, in its first half, more defeats than victories falling to our share ; whereas, in less than two campaigns, we conquered a great country and a peace, without the loss of a single battle or skirmish." I quote from Major-General G. W. Cullum's preface to Biographical Register of the Officers and Graduates of the United States Military Academy—a most valuable contribution to our Nation's history.

I have mentioned Iowa was admitted as a State, December 28, 1846. In 1841 it was a wilderness. Except a very small south-east corner, the Sacx and Foxes occupied the southern portion, the Sioux the northern portion, and the Winnebagoes a strip fifty miles wide, called the Neutral Territory between these tribes. From 1861 to 1865 Iowa furnished 100,000 men, bearing arms, to the Union Army. I suppose such a growth to be unparalleled in the history of the world.

Wisconsin was admitted May 29, 1848. California was admitted September 9, 1850. Minnesota was admitted May 11, 1858.

In 1857, Cyrus W. Field, Peter Cooper, and others laid the first Atlantic telegraph cable. The message of the Queen of England, the amiable Victoria, to the President of the United States, was transmitted August 16, 1858.

Oregon was admitted February 14, 1859. Kansas, January 29, 1861.

On the succeeding fourth of July our Flag by law bore thirty-four stars in its Union. A flag bearing these devices is in the possession of the American Geographical Society. It shows how an energetic people can carry out the description Manilius gave of the Lyre of Orpheus : " Nunc Sidera Ducit." As we watch the stars of Heaven, they seem only to pass from East to West ; but these stars, representing the new constellation, have wandered from their orbit, but have not yet been lost.

In 1838, they went with Wilkes' Expedition to a higher latitude toward the Southern Pole than the American flag ever went before in the Antarctic regions. De Haven, in command of the Grinnell Expedition, in search of Sir John Franklin, took them to a higher latitude in the northern regions than any other flag had ever been, but the stars of that flag did not grow dim in the Polar winter. Dr. Kane took them with another expedition to a still higher northern latitude ; they caught there the glow of the Aurora Borealis. With Dr. Hayes, in the same flag, they went 37 miles higher toward the Northern Pole than an American flag, or any other flag, had ever been.

West Virginia was admitted June 19, 1863. Nevada was admitted October 31, 1864. Nebraska was admitted March 1, 1867. Colorado was admitted August 1, 1876.

In the meantime, our flag was made more brilliant by the light thrown upon it by authors, painters, poets, sculptors, and practical men who have " endowed humanity with new and numerous inventions " — Gordon, Belknap, Bancroft, Hildreth, J. C. Hamilton, Cooper, Irving, Sparks, Ticknor, etc., as to the history of our own country ; Prescott, Motley, etc., as to the history of other lands ; Story, Curtis, Wheaton, Halleck, etc., in the departments of municipal and international law ; Irving, Cooper, Hawthorne, Holmes, Emerson, and a host of others in the lighter departments of literature ; Willis, Fitz Green Halleck, Bryant, Longfellow, Whittier, etc., in poetry; West, Weir, Alston, Trumbull, Peale, Church, Bierstadt, and Huntington, etc., as artists; Crawford and Powers, etc., as sculptors; Terry and Grey in botany; Audubon in Ornithology; Astor, Lenox, Peter Cooper, Vanderbilt, Vassar, Cornell, and many others who have so munificently endowed colleges, libraries, and hospitals; McCormick in his mower and reaper; Elias Howe in his sewing machine; and Hoe in his wonderful improvements of the printing press, which has enabled us to have our profusion of books, magazines, and newspapers—these last the sentinels on the watch-towers of Liberty.

I have purposely refrained from dwelling upon the internecine struggle, which cost us, North and South, 1,000,000 of men, killed and disabled, and probably $6,000,000,000 of material wealth. You all know the indomitable courage and brilliant soldiership displayed on both sides—the deeds of prowess by land and sea. How many hearts also of mothers and widows and orphans bled, and are still bleeding. How Lincoln fell. How all men in this land, this day, stand, not only before God, but in the Eye of the Law, the perfection of human reason, "free and equal." How though in a century many stars have been added, there is no Pleiad lost from the constellation of our Flag.

Like the little colony planted by a woman on Rhode Island, under the auspices of that great man Roger Williams, we have still, as set forth in its seal, the sheaf of arrows for enemies if they will, but we have also, in our right hand, the motto, "Amor Vincet Omnia."

Francis Lord Bacon said in his last will and testament: "For my name and memory, I leave it to men's charitable speeches, and to foreign nations and to the next age." We owe him a great debt. The world owes him a great debt. Socrates, Plato, and all the school-men, were impracticables. Bacon's philosophy was practicable. I have a profound respect for practical men, wherever found. They have made our country what it is. Bacon's philosophy was "to endow continually the human race with new faculties and powers of

employing them." "To suggest new ideas and the appli-
cation of them." "To work efficaciously to relieve human
life from its ills." Lord Macaulay says the key to his doc-
trine, which was fruit, was Utility and Progress. As a nation,
whosoever visited our late Centennial Exhibition, or has seen
it as reproduced in print, cannot but admit that though the
youngest of the nations, we have not been behind the oldest
in doing honor, practically, to the name and memory of
Francis Bacon, the Philosopher. As a nation, in introducing
Arbitration instead of the Sword, "Ultima ratio Regum,"
"the last resort of Kings," in international difficulties, we
have done honor to his name, Ethically and Politically. It
was to General Ulysses S. Grant, a West Point man, a man
of the sword, as Executive of the Nation, the world owes
this step in Utility and Progress and Peace. There are, this
day, the Centennial of its adoption, thirty-seven stars in the
union of our Flag, to be altered to thirty-eight stars July 4,
1877, because of the admission of Colorado. As in the Milky
Way in the heavens, other fixed stars, soon to take their
place there, are glimmering through the distance.

I close with the words of Joseph Rodman Drake:

> " When freedom from her mountain height
>   Unfurled her standard to the air,
> She tore the azure robe of night,
>   And set the stars of glory there !
> She mingled with its gorgeous dyes
> The milky baldric of the skies,
> And striped its pure, celestial white
> With streakings of the morning light ;
> Then from his mansion in the sun
> She called her eagle bearer down,
> And gave into his mighty hand
> The symbol of her chosen land !

> " Majestic monarch of the cloud !
>   Who rear'st aloft thy regal form,
> To hear the tempest-trumpings loud,
> And see the lightning lances driven,
>   When strive the warriors of the storm,
> And rolls the thunder-drum of heaven !

Child of the sun ! to thee 'tis given
To guard the banner of the free,
To hover in the sulphur smoke,
To ward away the battle stroke,
And bid its blendings shine afar,
Like rainbows on the cloud of war,
    The harbingers of victory.

" Flag of the brave ! thy folds shall fly,
The sign of hope and triumph high !
When speaks the signal trumpet tone,
And the long line comes gleaming on :
(E'er yet the life-blood, warm and wet,
Has dimmed the glistening bayonet,)
Each soldier eye shall brightly turn
To where thy sky-born glories burn,
And as his springing steps advance
Catch war and vengeance from the glance,
And when the cannon-mouthings loud
Heave in wild wreaths the battle shroud,
And gory sabres rise and fall,
Like shoots of flame on midnight's pall ;
Then shall the meteor-glances glow,
    And cowering foes shall sink beneath
Each gallant arm that strikes below
    That lovely messenger of death.

" Flag of the seas ! on ocean wave
Thy stars shall glitter o'er the brave ;
When death, careering on the gale,
Sweeps darkly round the bellied sail,
And frighted waves rush wildly back,
Before the broadside's reeling rack,
Each dying wanderer of the sea
Shall look at once to heaven and thee,
And smile to see thy splendors fly
In triumph o'er his closing eye.
Flag of the free hearts' hope and home
    By angel hands to valor given ;
Thy stars have lit the welkin dome
    And all thy hues were born of heaven !
Forever float that standard sheet !
    Where breathes the foe but falls before us ?
With freedom's soil beneath our feet
    And freedom's banner streaming o'er us ? "

SCHUYLER HAMILTON.

CPSIA information can be obtained
at www.ICGtesting.com
Printed in the USA
BVHW041214300119
539043BV00033B/1911/P

9 781333 027728